THE ARTEMIS PROGRAM

SIMON PIERCE

PowerKiDS press

Published in 2025 by The Rosen Publishing Group, Inc.
2544 Clinton Street, Buffalo, NY 14224

First Edition

Editor: Jennifer Lombardo
Book Design: Rachel Rising

Photo Credits: Cover https://en.wikipedia.org/wiki/File:Xemu-eva-Artemis.jpg; cover, pp. 1, 3–32 KK.KICKIN/ Shutterstock.com; p. 5 Elena11/Shutterstock.com; pp. 6, 9 Dima Zel/Shutterstock.com; p. 7 Ramunas Bruzas/ Shutterstock.com; p. 8 https://en.m.wikipedia.org/wiki/File:GATEWAY_(Moon_Space_Station).jpg; p. 10 https:// commons.wikimedia.org/wiki/File:Space_Launch_System_-_SLS.jp; p. 11 3Dsculptor/Shutterstock.com; p. 12 cfg1978/Shutterstock.com; p. 13 Sahel Fahmi/Shutterstock.com; p. 15 https://en.wikipedia.org/wiki/File:Sally_Ride_ (1984).jpg; p. 16 https://en.m.wikipedia.org/wiki/File:NASA_Artemis_Gateway_logo.png; p. 17 https://commons. wikimedia.org/wiki/File:Full_view_of_Gateway_(4k_0).jpg; p. 18 Mubashir Abbas Zaidi/Shutterstock.com; p. 19 MUSTAFA YANAR/Shutterstock.com; p. 21 luckyluke007/Shutterstock.com; p. 23 Dotted Yeti/Shutterstock.com; p. 24 https://en.wikipedia.org/wiki/File:Artemis_program_(original_with_wordmark).svg; p. 25 https://roundupreads.jsc. nasa.gov/roundup/2058; p. 26 muratart/Shutterstock.com; p. 27 Stag Photo and Video/Shutterstock.com; p. 28 Keith J Finks/Shutterstock.com; p. 29 NASA images/Shutterstock.com.

Library of Congress Cataloging-in-Publication Data

Names: Pierce, Simon, author.
Title: The Artemis mission / Simon Pierce.
Description: Buffalo, NY : PowerKids Press, [2025] | Series: Mission
    control | Includes bibliographical references and index.
Identifiers: LCCN 2024035637 | ISBN 9781499449792 (library binding) | ISBN
    9781499449785 (paperback) | ISBN 9781499449808 (ebook)
Subjects: LCSH: Artemis Program (U.S.)--Juvenile literature. | Space flight
    to the moon--Juvenile literature. | Moon--Exploration--Juvenile
    literature.
Classification: LCC TL799.M6 P55 2025 | DDC 629.45/4--dc23/eng/20240814
LC record available at https://lccn.loc.gov/2024035637

Manufactured in the United States of America

CPSIA Compliance Information: Batch #CWPK25. For further information contact Rosen Publishing at 1-800-237-9932.

CONTENTS

BACK TO THE MOON

On July 20, 1969, Neil Armstrong became the first human to set foot on our planet's moon, thanks to **NASA**'s Apollo 11 mission. From that year until 1972, more Apollo missions took place. Overall, 12 people—all men—have walked on the moon. However, after 1972, the moon missions were canceled due to their high cost.

In the early 2000s, NASA announced that it would prepare to return to the moon. This mission, called Artemis, has several different goals. The most ambitious of these is to set up a permanent base on the moon. This would serve as a gateway for astronauts on an eventual mission to Mars. It would also allow scientists to test new technology in relatively close space before putting it to use farther from home.

NASA KNOWLEDGE

In Greek mythology, Apollo was the god of the sun. His twin sister, Artemis, was the goddess of the moon.

Because there is no wind on the moon to blow its **regolith** around, the astronauts' footprints are still there.

THE LUNAR GATEWAY

Artemis's Lunar Gateway—usually shortened to just "Gateway"—is a space station that will remain in orbit around the moon. Astronauts will be able to live there while they conduct scientific research onboard. They will also make trips to the moon's surface to collect samples to study. For this reason, an important part of Gateway is its Human Landing System (HLS). These are smaller spacecraft that will take people and cargo from Gateway to the moon and back.

The International Space Station (ISS) always has several astronauts living on it. However, Gateway will not be continuously occupied. Astronauts will make short trips, and Gateway will have instruments on board to conduct research even when no one is there.

BUILT IN SPACE

Gateway has not been built yet. NASA is working with the European Space Agency (ESA), Canadian Space Agency (CSA), Japan Aerospace Exploration Agency (JAXA), and the Mohammed Bin Rashid Space Centre of the United Arab Emirates to build the craft. Some parts will be assembled on the ground. Those will be launched into space no earlier than 2025 and connected later by astronauts.

Gateway will have two places for astronauts to rest, exercise, and eat. It will also have cargo storage, research labs, and places for visiting ships to **dock**.

Large ships can't get too close to shore, so passengers take a smaller ship called a tender. The HLS will act as Gateway's tenders. However, unlike a ship's tender, the HLS will be designed for humans to live in for up to a week.

A CLOSER LOOK

Gateway will be made up of several large parts called modules. The main module is called the Habitation and Logistics Outpost (HALO). This is where the command center will be. From here, astronauts will be able to control Gateway. HALO will power the other modules. It is also designed to **monitor** and regulate certain things, such as solar **radiation** levels, temperature, and oxygen.

Another major part of Gateway is called International Habitation (I-HAB). This will be where most of the astronauts spend their time. It will have living quarters as well as science labs. The third module is called ESPRIT. It will have the tools that astronauts on Gateway need to communicate with Earth and with the astronauts on the moon's surface. This is also where Gateway can be refueled.

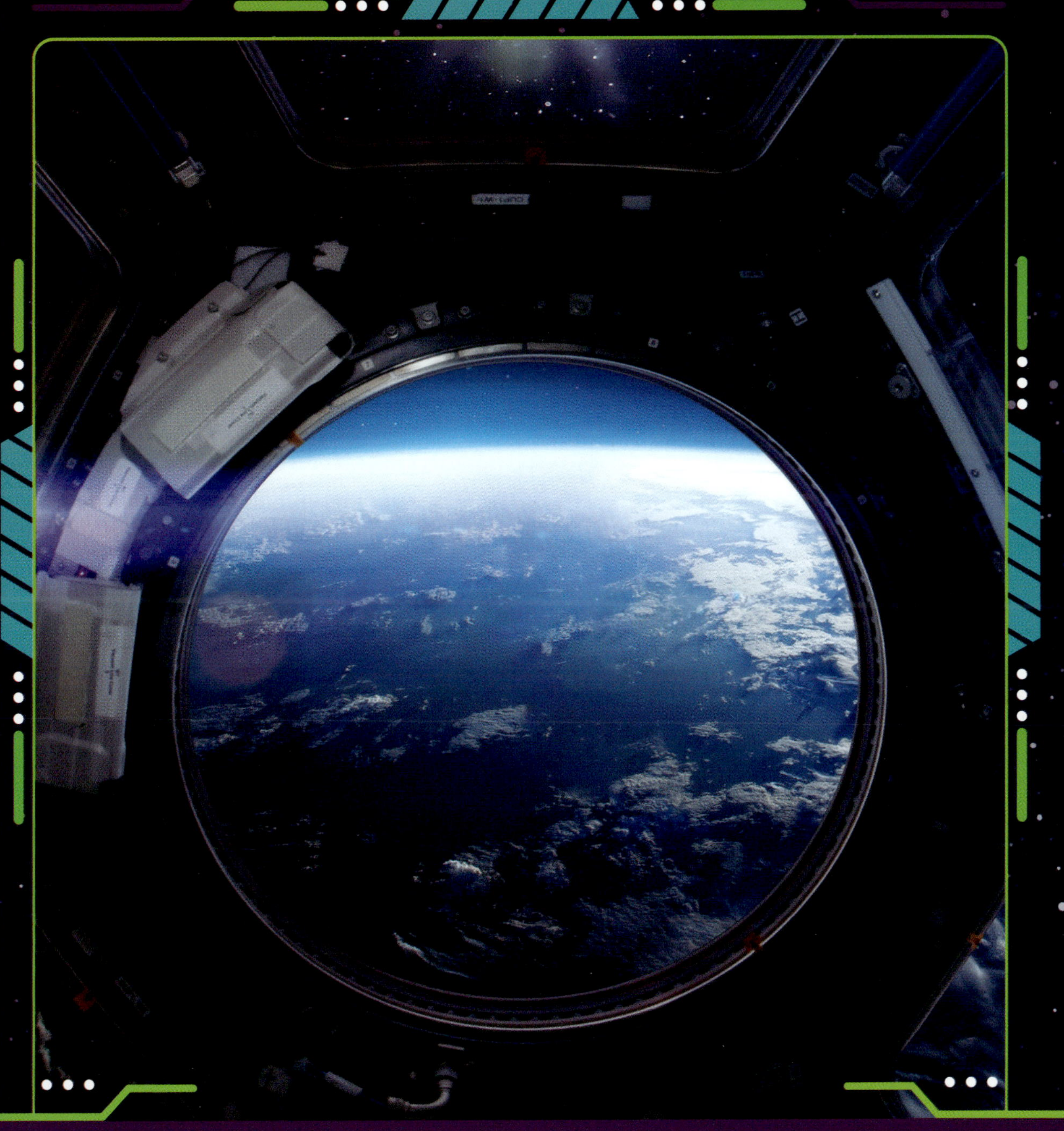

The ISS has a large window from which astronauts can see breathtaking views. On Gateway, ESPRIT will have a similar window.

SPACE LAUNCH SYSTEM

All the pieces of Gateway will be sent into orbit on the Space Launch System (SLS). This kind of huge rocket is made to carry heavy equipment into space. As of 2024, it is the only rocket in the world powerful enough to take people and cargo straight to the moon in one launch.

The SLS will carry the *Orion* spacecraft into space. This ship will have four astronauts on board. Once in space, the *Orion* will separate from the SLS and dock at Gateway. The astronauts will then be able to exit *Orion* and enter Gateway. When they are ready to return home, the astronauts will travel back to Earth in *Orion*. After it reenters the atmosphere, several **parachutes** will open so *Orion* can safely float down to land in the ocean.

The SLS is taller than the Statue of Liberty.

MULTIPLE MISSIONS

The Artemis program will not be completed all at once. Instead, NASA has a timeline of multiple missions. This will help make sure that when astronauts travel to Gateway, as many problems as possible have been worked out.

The first mission, Artemis I, was completed in 2022. It was unmanned, meaning there were no people on *Orion*. This first mission was meant to expose any problems that might endanger a crew. The SLS launched with *Orion* in November. The trip went according to plan: *Orion* separated from the SLS, circled the moon twice, then returned to Earth and splashed down in the Pacific Ocean off the coast of California. *Orion* was recovered by NASA to be used again in future flights.

THE MOONIKINS

Artemis I held three **mannequins**, nicknamed "Moonikins," that were dressed in the spacesuits that real astronauts will wear on later Artemis missions. The reason they were on board was to test the spacesuits in space conditions before any person wore them.

NASA engineers also placed sensors on the Moonikins that would let them monitor what the Moonikins were experiencing. This way, if any problems came up—for example, if the oxygen level in the cabin dropped suddenly—the engineers would know about it and be able to figure out the cause.

Along with the Moonikins, there were two toy "astronauts" on *Orion*. The ESA sent Shaun the Sheep, and NASA sent Snoopy.

NEHT STEPS

The Artemis I mission went as expected, with no major problems. Artemis II will be much the same, but with four human astronauts onboard. The astronauts will spend up to 10 days in space, collecting more information and testing what *Orion* can do.

Artemis III will last 30 days. Again, four astronauts will travel into space on *Orion*. This time, however, *Orion* will dock with the parts of Gateway that are already orbiting the moon. Two astronauts will land on the moon for the first time since 1972. They will spend almost a week on the surface, collecting samples. The other two astronauts will stay on *Orion* for that time. When the first two astronauts return to *Orion*, the whole crew will return to Earth.

NASA KNOWLEDGE

The two astronauts who will go to the moon's surface during the Artemis III mission will be the first woman and the first person of color to set foot on the moon.

NASA didn't allow women to be astronauts until 1978. In 1983, Sally Ride became the first American woman to go to space. By this time, two female Russian cosmonauts had already been to space.

In addition to more astronauts, Artemis IV will deliver Gateway's living quarters to space. The astronauts will connect it to the rest of the space station and be the first crew to live on Gateway for a short time. As with Artemis III, two astronauts will spend a week on the moon's surface. The other two will stay on Gateway, conducting science experiments. The Gateway astronauts will complete one orbit of the moon before picking up the other two crew members and returning to Earth in *Orion*.

Artemis V will deliver another module, or part, to Gateway. The mission will be essentially the same as Artemis IV. Beyond that, NASA and the other space agencies have no definite plans yet, but they are hoping to continue the Artemis missions.

SHIFTING TIMELINES

As of 2024, the timeline for the Artemis missions is as follows:

- Artemis II: no earlier than September 2025
- Artemis III: no earlier than September 2026
- Artemis IV: no earlier than 2028
- Artemis V: unscheduled

This timeline is **tentative**. Many things can happen to delay a space mission. Artemis I was originally scheduled for 2016. It was pushed back to 2021 and then again to 2022. Four launches in 2022 were canceled due to bad weather and other problems before the launch finally went off as planned in November. Artemis II has already been pushed back from its original planned date of November 2024.

This picture shows what Gateway will look like when it is fully assembled.

SOLVING PROBLEMS

Although Artemis I went as planned, no mission is perfect. NASA and ESA engineers got an opportunity to find and address an issue that could have caused bigger problems on later missions. They noticed an **anomaly** with one of the power conditioning units. This piece of equipment is designed to take in energy from the sun, convert it into usable solar power, and distribute the power to the parts of the ship that need it.

The power conditioning unit has components, or parts, on it to stop it from flooding parts of the ship with too much power. During the mission, engineers noticed that the ship automatically switched open some of those components. They quickly got to work, figured out what had happened, and fixed the problem so it wouldn't happen again.

FUTURE PROBLEMS

Space engineers also have to think about how to solve problems that haven't come up yet. For example, some people have raised concerns about moon dust. The regolith on the moon is very thick and sticky, and astronauts will track it into Gateway when they return from the moon's surface. If this regolith starts flying around, it could jam equipment and cause breathing problems for the astronauts.

To address this problem, engineers are working on ways to **decontaminate** the astronauts between the HLS and Gateway. They are also designing a dust-collecting payload for Gateway. This means any dust that gets into Gateway would be sucked up into a container, and the container would be **jettisoned** when it gets full.

Although it doesn't look like it from Earth, the moon's surface is very dusty.

MAJOR GOALS

The Artemis missions have several goals. Some are very ambitious, while others are easy to achieve. For example, one of the goals is to allow the first person of color and the first woman to land on the surface of the moon. Although those astronauts have not yet been chosen, the space agencies working on Artemis have a large pool of very good candidates to choose from.

Another goal that has already been met is for NASA to partner with private companies. SpaceX, Boeing, and others have already signed contracts and provided NASA with materials for the Artemis missions. Because NASA is a government agency, its budget is determined by Congress. Working with private companies can help NASA stretch its budget further.

NASA KNOWLEDGE

As of 2024, NASA has already run into serious budget problems. The SLS alone is incredibly expensive to use, which means future missions may be more limited than NASA had first expected them to be.

Shown here is a test spacecraft SpaceX built for NASA. In addition to partnering with NASA, SpaceX is working on building its own spacecraft to send people to space for short vacations.

ONWARD TO MARS

One of the more difficult goals to achieve is creating technology that can keep astronauts alive and healthy on longer missions that take place deeper in space. According to NASA, Gateway is just the first step in a plan to send astronauts to Mars. In addition to gathering more information about the moon, astronauts will be testing the spacesuits and spacecraft to see how well they work. Engineers will make changes where necessary so this equipment is safe and functional for a much longer trip.

This long-term goal will likely not even begin to have firm plans for several decades. First, all the Artemis missions will need to be completed. As this timeline keeps being pushed back and NASA's plans keep changing, the project is in danger of being canceled by Congress.

NASA KNOWLEDGE

Plans for a manned Mars mission have been proposed and canceled multiple times since the 1950s. Cost and politics are two major obstacles that always come up.

A MAJOR CHALLENGE

Sending humans to Mars is easy. Sending them to Mars safely and bringing them back safely, on the other hand, is a problem NASA may not be ready to solve yet—or possibly ever. Although Artemis will help NASA identify and solve certain problems, there are some that will never come up on such a short mission. For example, although NASA can calculate the amount of time and fuel it will take to get to Mars, unexpected obstacles could cause delays and fuel shortages.

Another problem is that the farther away from Earth astronauts get, the longer it will take to send messages back and forth. In an emergency, astronauts could be waiting as long as 20 minutes for their distress signal to reach Earth and another 20 minutes for the response.

This picture shows one artist's idea of what a base on Mars might look like.

CHALLENGES TO ARTEMIS

Although the Artemis program has only just begun, it is already facing serious challenges. One of the biggest is its cost. The program was already expensive, but NASA has changed the requirements several times since its budget was approved. Each change has driven the cost higher. For example, in 2019, NASA made deals with two private companies. One company called Maxar would make the Power and Propulsion Element (PPE), while another called Northrop Grumman would make the HALO.

By November 2020, NASA had decided to launch these two parts together instead of separately. NASA stated that this change would decrease costs by requiring only one launch instead of two. However, the decision meant changes needed to be made to the design of the PPE, which made the cost higher in the end.

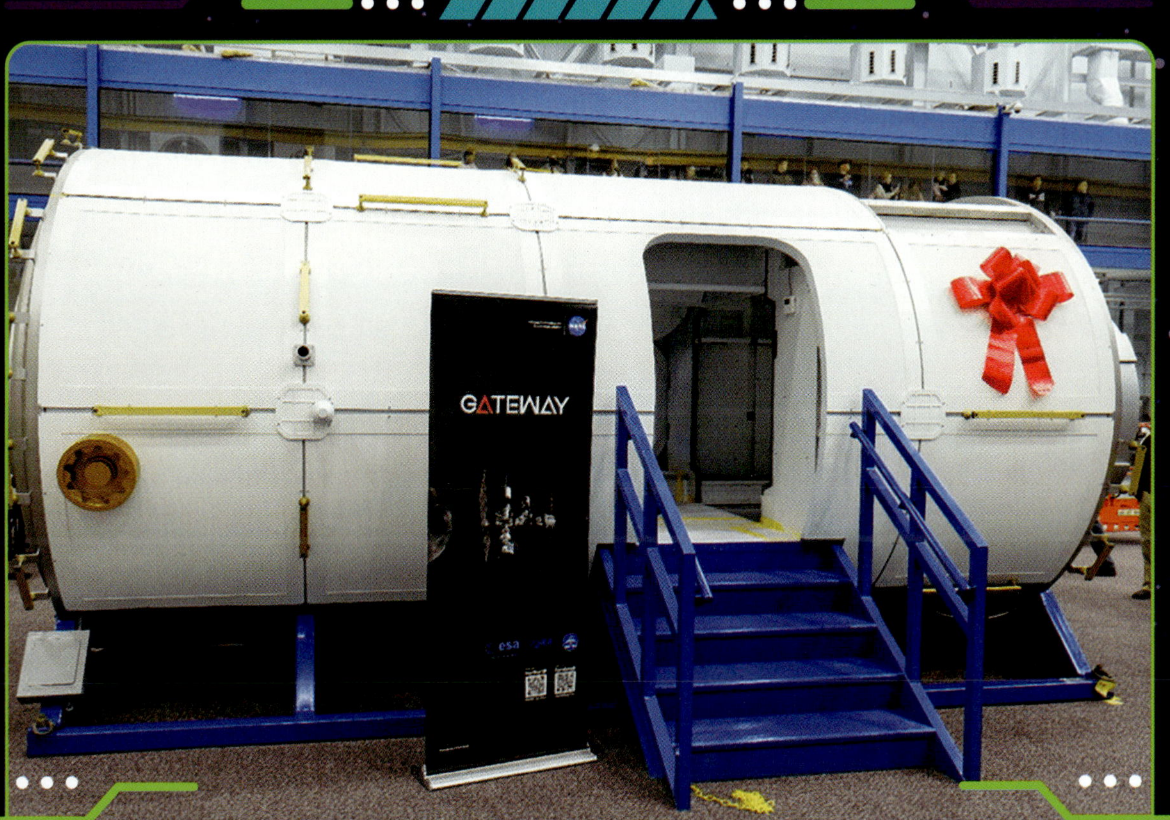

In 2023, Northrop Grumman delivered a **prototype** of HALO to NASA. Since it was delivered a few days before Christmas, the company added a red bow to the prototype to make it seem like a Christmas gift to NASA.

Not all of Artemis's challenges are caused by NASA's decisions. Some have been completely out of the agency's control. For example, the COVID-19 pandemic that started in 2020 delayed engineers' ability to work on some parts of the project.

Artemis has also faced some opposition from the public. One of NASA's stated goals for Artemis is to find and possibly mine rare minerals on the moon. This link to economic advancement has helped give it support in Congress. However, many Americans as well as other world governments have expressed concern and even outrage over this idea. The moon belongs to Earth, not to one single country. Some people are worried that mining the moon could cause problems on Earth, such as a war over the moon's resources.

An isotope of helium, helium-3, is much more commonly found on the moon than on Earth. This isotope can be used to create nuclear energy on Earth.

LOOKING FORWARD

The future of the Artemis program remains uncertain. As of 2024, the program is set to continue as planned. However, it seems as though NASA will continue to face challenges. It will likely have to continue to prove that its program is worth the cost. It will also likely have to continue making changes to its spacecraft after each mission to make sure everything runs smoothly on future missions.

In spite of these challenges, NASA and other space agencies remain hopeful. They are committed to making sure space travel is safe for astronauts, even if that costs a lot of money. They also believe strongly in exploring space to learn more about our solar system. For NASA, the search for knowledge is priceless.

NASA hopes the Artemis mission will pave the way for exploration deeper into our solar system and, in the far future, possibly more of the galaxy.

GLOSSARY

anomaly: Something different, abnormal, strange, or not easily described.

decontaminate: To get rid of something that soils, stains, or infects people or things that come into contact with it.

dock: In space, to join one ship to another.

jettison: To throw goods overboard from a ship, aircraft, or spacecraft.

mannequin: A form representing the human figure used especially for displaying clothes.

monitor: To carefully observe over a period of time.

NASA: National Aeronautics and Space Administration.

parachute: A large, umbrella-shaped piece of fabric that slows the descent of someone or something.

payload: Something carried by a vehicle in addition to what is necessary for its operation.

prototype: A model on which future items are patterned.

radiation: Energy put out as waves or particles.

regolith: The dust that lies on top of solid rock on the moon.

tentative: Highly likely to change.